M000201502

THE ALTAR OF THE ONLY WORLD

Sharanya Manivannan's first book of poems, *Witchcraft*, was described by Ng Yi-Sheng in *The Straits Times* as 'sensuous and spiritual, delicate and dangerous and as full as the moon reflected in a knife'. Her short story collection, *The High Priestess Never Marries*, won a South Asia Laadli Media and Advertising Award for Gender Sensitivity (Best Book – Fiction) and was shortlisted for the TATA Lit Live! First Book Award (Fiction). She has also written a picture book for children, *The Ammuchi Puchi*.

She was specially commissioned to write and perform a poem at the 2015 Commonwealth Day Observance in London. She is also known for her long-running column, *The Venus Flytrap*, in *The New Indian Express*. Born in India in 1985, Sharanya grew up in Sri Lanka and Malaysia, and has lived in Chennai since 2007.

THE
ALTAR
OF
THE
ONLY
WORLD

SHARANYA
MANIVANNAN

HarperCollins *Publishers* India

First published in hardback in India by
HarperCollins *Publishers* India
A-75, Sector 57, Noida, Uttar Pradesh 201301, India
www.harpercollins.co.in

2 4 6 8 10 9 7 5 3 1

P-ISBN: 978-93-5277-104-2
E-ISBN: 978-93-5277-105-9

Typeset in Goudy Old Style at
SÜRYA, New Delhi

Printed and bound at
Thomson Press (India) Ltd

For Veenapani Chawla

CONTENTS

~

~

~

Hanuman

The man with the heart that grew armour
took my breasts in his palms
and torn asunder, there, was
mine.

I took his bloody hands and
looked him in the eyes.
I am not a woman who must
prepare for sadness, I said.
I am not a woman who
cannot tell the place of the
original sin from the evil of its twin.

Crack me open, I said.
Take from me all I can give.

The god in me saw the god
in you. Our demons
saw each other too.

My heart is a cactus.
My heart has been waiting
for your stone. I'm as opaque
as the water
waiting within, flooded full
and capable
of unimaginable giving.

Come, ugly one.
Bring me your dirty paws
and your bearded countenance,
your blueness, your bliss. Bring me
nothing if that is all you are
capable of bearing.
I'll take it all.
I'll take every last
bulletproof
offering.

Sun-swallower

During the eclipse, it was rumoured
that the wildfire in your belly was
the only known source of light
in the universe.

The darkness you found me in
was only the penumbra of the
darkness you would
plunge into me.

What gravity you wielded then.
I came to you not knowing that
the light you held
within yourself was also
the light you withheld
from the world.

There was already darkness in me.

And if not light itself, then
afterglow, and though scorched
forever with the analemma
of your passage,

in the cosmos of my body,
always room for
another sun.

Mirrors

I saw a therukoothu dancer
spinning in the sun
today.

Every mirror along
his arms caught the sun
as he spun,
throwing it in small
constellations against
the shadows of the
courtyard.

And come unspooled in
his whirling was the memory
of a different dervish, and how
the compass arrows of my need
had spun with him then, shimmering,
possessed and scattering light, until
I could no longer see when
you gathered them up and
flung them, like cowries
from the palm of a
soothsayer. I ruptured
against your walls. I shone.

And when he
straightened his spine
and began to sing to
the goddess of rain, his
feet finally still against the earth,
I thought again of what she told me
that day, during the eclipse,
in her garden of datura –

Never love a man with more faces
than a hall of mirrors. He will
never be able to tear his eyes away
long enough to look at you,
a luminous thing, blinded by
the dark gravity of your love.

Secret Theatres

Tonight, the chhau dancer has a moon on his back,
and he clasps each of its crescent wingtips
above his head like an angel holding its horns.

When I said that I have looked for you in the bodies
of others, this is what I meant: these martial stances,
these masks, the way his shoulderblades convulse

in tandem with a shuddering drum, the way he raises
a foot to the level of the eye. Some of us are forged
salamandrine, enduring the universe with no more

than the will to be reborn. Others must wear falconry
hoods, and sometimes, when even I can no longer bear
to see, I think of you: once, your head in your hands

in a gesture of mourning, that night at the beginning
of the year of broken idols when a beautiful costumed
man ripped his chest open and showed you that secret

theatre, that solitaire, the hooked bijou of my heart.
Since then, the cosmos has been without choreography.
The seraph on stage unsheathes his trident. I wrap myself

in a serape of sadness and wonder how many dancers
I have watched on how many nights since; how many
I have torn my gaze from to beseech the sky,
as though the night numbered among
its many stars the zodiac of your eyes.

Chhaya

All night I translated for you from the book of shadow-dancing. 'They call this *the theatre of skin*,' I whispered, hand within hand in the darkness of the amphitheatre. All night, I traced your salt to the stardust of its origins. 'Our word for shadow is their word for light.' I was a mercenary then, seduced by the costume of the trickster, a fabulist who would betray the empire to tell the truth. There were whole countries behind me, a trail of tears and relinquished ornaments, and art was the red yarn that led me back into and out of the world. You were a georama of constellations, and I didn't know yet how I would have to watch your every fall. That night I could believe it – that all the anguish that had transpired had happened only to my shadow. While my true nature – never surrendered – had never been interrupted of its fierce smoulder, was always and ever would be an absolute and sempiternal light.

Venus of the Diaspora

There were no lodestars in the house of love
on the quiet morning of the fall of light.

Grief spun through space like a meteorite.

Worlds moved as devotion refused to bow
to laws untrue, so fierce that even now
when exiles string their syllables and write
she glows luciferous in chthonic night;
lit from deep within, not just from above.

It's the dark that cradles the stars apart.
It's great loss that serves as beauty's spindle.

Gather the cure-songs, the ancient symbols;
she'll scry the myths in a mirror of quartz.
Illuminate the obscured, rekindle
the holy, O lady of largest heart.

Southern Cross

Because we cannot take these bodies into heaven,
we must ground them here in the arable of
the afterglow.

Tooth and hair, sweat and musk.
Constellations to stardust –

I remember you.
I re-member you.

Here, hold still, here is the crux of it,
the point of entry, the continental drift.

Let me taste in turn the holy stations:

      shoulder   shoulder
           mouth
           south

centres of pilgrimage,
exalted in perfect equilibrium,

and save for last that
    sun-drunk supernova,
conflagration
within your ribs.

Distant Star

You slid a pin into my body and
brooched me at a distance, a dwarf

star snared against a night on the
other side of the universe, imagining

yourself a lapidary, setting diamond
upon obsidian, holding your tongue

so that the hooks in your mouth
would not fall. You believe you sleep

the sleep of the guiltless, but it is only
the sleep of the damned, and on the

day when you wake to the sight of me,
ascending before dawn, a planet blue-

burning and beautiful, it is the stones
of your eyes that will sear you, it is your

pins you will swallow, javelined by the
serration of every word you left unsaid.

Light Years

There are still hours of the night
    when I can sense you, in the house
you have built at the end of eternity,

counting the moments between
    each glimmer of a pulse of light

I had left burning in the far reaches
of a season beyond reversion, when

    I had stood still so my coordinates
would not change, believing the
    universe an incalculable

territory, and you, a pilgrim guided
    by the votives of a thousand
loved and surrendered suns.

That was a long time ago. When
    I made love to you it was with
the memory of each star
that had died to become our bodies

and when I let you go I kept every
    map, every myth, imprinted
in aether as in chassis.

I held you across space

for as long as I could, in a sinusoid
    of dimming lanterns,
orbits in disorder, legend
    without chronology –

and time, though measured in light,
divides itself only in darkness.

Tagelied

The goddess unknotted her cincture
under the aegis of noctilucent clouds,
and the night passed like a reverie –
your breath in my ear, a newly baptised
asterism, the wine. Perhaps I was her sibyl,
perhaps you were her object of illumination,
but how quickly the world turned under us,

so that by the time you finally tendered me
the sky, the morning star was a rose.
I wanted to be deeply lost in you,
to become something more than
a recursive memory, some cosmic
mirage, a pulsar singing into oblivion.

I wanted something other than
myth and antemeridian promise.
I wanted the taste of your fingers
in my mouth for all eternity. But how
did I not read the line of that horizon –
love is a form of phosphorescence,
a shyness,   slow to cast its light,
but slower still to unfurl its shadow.

Ravanahatha

The universe is made of strings,
and that night under the udumbara
my body became a lute
as I watched you play,
and my fall
became
grace.

Dark Moon

Mouth within mouth,
breath within breath,

scintilla of skin in the
    light of eclipse –

hold me as you held
    your shadow – that night

on the reef of dreams the universe
    became a spicebox of beads,

the coral and turquoise moon
    hanging low in its hammock

an earring resting on
    the collarbone of the coast.

Shape-shifter

In those years of hallucinatory dreaming
I was convinced that when you returned,
it would be in some inconceivable form.

A trick of light, a shadowless being,
a beauty so startling that mirrors
would withdraw, opaque as the winter
lakes of northern countries.

I looked for you everywhere.

I thought you were coded in the wind –
a sunburst, a falling star, a golden deer.
My longing drawn taut as a bowstring,
I could have sighted you in any guise.

One grows watchful in the wilderness,
believes everything possible.

I would have taken you in any shape,
any apparition you arrived in, man or beast,
illusion or evidence, demon or god.
Any shape you could have come in.
If only you had come.

Echo

The forest captured the sound of your voice
as though within a conch. I held its chimera
to my ear and let it wrench through my life,
the way fools listen to humming shells
not recognizing the song of their own
blood-tide, not trusting their bodies
capable of encapsulating the sea.

Monsoon

This year, something in the smell of rain
brings to mind the nature of the light
without which you marauded that terrain,

each breath of yours an impulse of cordite,
your voice a chord that would not echo.
Though I catch myself still listening, tonight,

as though you might yet enter this tableau,
a raindrop palpitating the calm of still water.
I ache with memory blunt as an arrow.

Come without your weapons of slaughter.
The rock of my heart, igneous with pain,
softens to clay, calls for its poet, its potter.

And if it be your will to come here again,
return in deluge, submerge this floodplain.

Fulfilment

The wish-fulfilling tree
was a flame-of-the-forest
bleeding its petals
over the spine
of a woman

who had rather curved into stone
than to never have known
what it's like to be
loved lushly.

I didn't know yet what
desire was. I couldn't
tell it apart from mere
devotion.

But I sat to watch a little
while, as the world
breathed on her behalf:
petal by petal,
drip by drip.

Aurum

Heart-stealer, hermetic mirage,
how long before I could conceive

of you did you withhold yourself
from me? Never again may I know

desire like the one that turned molten
within me as the forest parted its

draperies to reveal you: velvet-pelted,
conch-bellied, precious-eyed, gold.

Pure gold. Dappled with jewels, radiant
like the path of moonlight on water.

Splendour itself, all those years of
nameless yearning, and then: alchemy.

For the rest of my days I will walk
with your crown of antlers on my

head, the inevitability of the hunt at
my hooves, and the memory of how

you tumbled from the brow of Orion
into my lap, and I held you at my

breasts, humming a stellar lullaby as
you turned to glitter in my blood.

Lustre

Even the huntress moon was
        jaundiced with gold
    in the delirium that came
at my first sight of you,
dear – my deer – dearest –

    rippling in the verdure like
a sentience under water, like
sunlight on a shattering mirror, like
    the thing I had wanted all my life
with no name by which to claim it.

Everywhere I turned – gilt.
Gilt on the borders of every foliole.
Gilt on the spines of each omen-singing cicada.
Gilt on the mud-motifs of my own feet
    after rainfall, so I circled and circled
    like someone on her own tail,
    or desperately in prayer.

                I chased you myself.
I chased you into the forest, forgetting
every line I lived by, a quiver of
    quicksilver aimed straight for
                            your ore.

Huntress

In the old days, blood was bought with blood.
We drove lances through bulls and
      drained them, strapped their skins
to our own to protect us from ourselves.

We drew our swords and crossed them.

Now there are no more rituals.
      There is no within,
      there is no without.
I am already here, ever in the wilderness.

I run a palm along the down
on a limb   and find spearheads at its tips.
   I straighten my spine and feel beneath me
a throbbing body, a burdened beast.

Two eyes closed while one never sleeps.
When there is nothing to flee, there is
      nothing to seek. I chased
   the rumour down
to its unlikeliest conclusion.

And here I stand, in the absence of sacrament.

I raise my cup to the heavens
and let the milky way fill my mouth.

Possession

And if you ask me now, I cannot tell you what came over me. I have called it by many names since – miracle, madness, myth, mistake – but at that time I only knew it as magic. Barefoot and consumed with grief, that winter in the forest sanctuary, I entered my mourning the way one enters water, trusting in gravity and in weightlessness. Who knows what had summoned him there. I only know that he too had arrived as I had, and under a sky shattered with stars, our orbits would chance and collide.

Nothing prepared me.

One by one each of my secret architectures, dismantled. Holiest communion, his thumb at the centre of my palm on that darkening highway, and me, a tremor caught between his thigh and his throat. His lips at the centre of my body. I imploded like a dark star.

The coast with no harbour where he left me, unanchored. I kept returning there, to the forest of pepper vines and burnt umber earth, a house of red bricks with its roof open to the light. I kept looking for something. I had seen it, in those moments of excavation, initiation. I had let it lift me into transcendence; let it lead me from death into immortality, from oblivion into original sin, from darkness into light.

That morning when the rain kissed every leaf, and I watched him walk on water, his feet leaving a trajectory of ripples. The omens of owls and winged things; a corona of monarch butterflies arching towards the moon. I am religious because I have known the grace that is the meeting of bodies, the sacraments of blood and breath. I have seen how rupture can reveal itself to be rapture. Lost in the slow helix of his body in mine, the only language left on my tongue was his name, natural as prayer. I took the talisman around his neck between my fingers and raised my eyes to his. I invoked the only word I still remembered, and called it baptism. I witnessed and blessed. I witnessed and blessed.

Nothing moved him.

I had marvelled at his penis in me. When it slipped out and he lay on his back, that final night, I had touched the wet warmth that covered it and said, 'All of this is me.' I had taken him into my mouth. I had let him break me open like birth.

That night in the theatre in the village when his god danced inside the body of a man and told him to go to me, bearing flowers, bearing flight.

Night-walker

Among all the terrible things
I have held within my body,
none was as unspeakable as
your absence from it.

For you who never came,
I ached among your company,
roaming amidst charnel-
dwellers and bier-sleepers,

befriending the broken, not yet
comprehending that deed is belief,
and no body who has glimpsed it
calls purgatory a performance.

It's no ordinary thing, night-
walker, to return from the dead.
Mutilation is not seamless,
even if healed with aurelian
gossamer. I have been there,

night-walker, out of longing
for you.

And I will never go back.
But now, and then, in
the most recondite of places,
I can reassemble the form
I made myself for you –

ormolu-husked,
serpent-tongued,
my cervine face,
my pavonine tail.

Talisman

In another life, in another
time of burning,
I pelted a black antelope
and allowed tiny creatures
to thrive and expire
in the stranglers of my hair,
my breath the stillness
before an arrow is released.

Sometimes I long for those dark hours
when the moon belonged only to me

     and I endured my exile
with a clear and naïve courage.

It was less than loneliness then –

    those crescent-cradled nights when
I would walk through   savage rain
and into unyielding caves
with nothing more than

the talisman of your
one thousand and one names
for company.

Each dewdrop
on my skin the memory
of how I drew your eyes to me,
    your reflection in a row
of gems like a denary
of heads around
my throat.

This Suffering

I painted my eyes and waited for you
　　at the anaretic hour of
the century of meteors.

The rain had lamented for years.
Even in that sunless season I could
decipher the east. Armfuls of
arrowheads, mud in my mouth,

fists of wet earth swallowed
without apprehension.

I painted my eyes and waited for you.
That house of red clay and mirrors
no more than a mirage.

A century of meteors.

　　The old myths of the eclipse
as the maw of a demon,

only a lover, starved in abandonment,
　　consuming every thing that might
retain the memory of this suffering.

Beloved pyromaniac, you cannot know
how I hungered for you then – the nights
I nearly burnt down the forest myself.

I could have eaten you alive if I had
sighted you on the horizon,

your starlit plough, your cratered
heart, your comet's tail.

Remember Me in Mud

Two routes between the city and the forest monastery:
    the road by the coast,
    the hilled boulevard of temples.

Take the one that lets you find me soonest.
Under my feet, something implacable in the earth,

    a collusion with the gathering storm to wipe
clean these tracks, the dust of this much displacement.
Forgive her. She is parched with grief.

And if you do not come in time,
remember me in harvest, in seeds sterile and sown,
in wind-carried pollen, in the first breach
    of buds in the new season.
Remember me in mud.

Disorientation

We arrived at the reef of dreams with
all our unharboured intentions bare
as trails of sea foam on a receding shore.

This is your freedom, you said.
The past is a delirious deceit,
and you have been denied passage.

I cannot carry you into the forest,
a vassal in your own dominion.
Do not follow me. Turn in any other
direction – *and I looked*, and to my east

was water, and to my west was withheld vision,
and the north was the country of your constraint
and the south was a burning reverie.

Your horses whimpered at your whip.
Your chariots left the coast a cut lip,
the moon an indecipherable mirage

as I staggered into the ocean
longing for the lumber of its weight.

The Unravelling

Would you believe me if I told you
    that in that
unmeasurable abandonment
I unlearned how to count? There

were things I survived only
    because their sums
were surmountable, while their
syntax came apart in my grasp

like a string of prayer beads
in a grip of desperate fervour,

the senses abdicating in terror

like republics left to the mercy
and cowardice of
a venal king.

A Country Contains Nothing

A country contains nothing,
only lines that partition
based on happenstance
beyond our control.

Only lines that partition
who we are from what claims us
beyond our control.
There's a circle wildly burning

who we are from what claims us,
a haemorrhage of borders.
There's a circle wildly burning.
But what I'd give to be inside.

A haemorrhage of borders,
based on happenstance.
What I'd give to be inside – even
if – a country contains nothing.

Insomnia

My body was the conch
    I carried back with me,
and now I drown each
night on this other shore,

the disappeared sea breaching
    upon my forehead
in beads of stinging salt.

We are nothing more
than the memory
of all the love
that has passed through us
in any direction.

Under a moon unclaimed by
    another, I incarnate the surge
as it ventures and recedes,
    ventures and recedes.

The weighted woodapple
    tree, the musk-wombed doe –
I remember them with envy.
Cakora birds that can
never know   love in the
lucidity of light.

My hair so fragrant that
bees clustered around it,
their murmur in my ears
the exact timbre
of dying stars.

We should never have left the island.

Each day more of its scent abandons me,
and my tongue grows coarser with desuetude.

I swallow its names
    as though to keep them
secret,   and at the first bleed of

dawn I slither into dreams of verdigris,
    a nine-jewelled heliocentrism,
and honey cascading down wild trees,
    down such wild and sinless sandal trees.

Carceral

If there is a way back into
that country, I will receive that road
wherever it deigns to meet me.

In another century I held gems
in my lower jaw and waited underwater
for a signal. Borders crossed in the
shadows of boats.

Here in the aperture between
history and memory, I languish
        within

a circle without a caesura

the lived regret   the forgotten escape

a gate that cannot be seen cannot be scaled
a girl who cannot be seen cannot be saved.

The forest has petrified into
a necropolis of statues.
There is rumour of a shortage of stars.
The nights darken and lengthen,
    madden with grief.

This heart will sink this body
if it turns any more to stone.

Firewife

When you did not come back for me,
I bit off my braid and walked
my heaviness to the river

and cursed the many ways I had
sought to hold you – how I had stood
bloodless under the victor's flag,

disarmed pillage, all my hopes quivering
mother-of-pearl in the moonlight.

Once, love was an unmarked territory,
a way to forge an uncommon ground.
Then, love lit a burning boundary,
and lifted its great wings in shame and

circled and circled and circled.

Death, Wearing All Her Glories

Death, wearing all her glories,
assumes her place at the table,
adorned by the carcanet of the
evening star.

In my porch a swing moves without passenger

a worn garland of jasmine hangs
on the window arabesque.

I say a rosary for children
    we will never name,
hold their umbilical cords between
my teeth and braid them into my hair

    and then I wait for you
in the first minutes of a darkening earth,

as everything I have ever loved begins
to materialize on the horizon, illumed by

the diamond in my nostril
twinkling
all night, all night

Beauty

the mutilated one

You came to me at sunset, so that at first
you could not discern cicatrix from skin.
The hour of occultation painted
this face orange and black
like a theyyam dancer
or a tigerlily.

And you asked me – how do you breathe
– and I said *the heart* – and you
had no need then to ask
how I listened.

But it was you who ached with even a whisper.

When we lifted you out of the river
your hair was constellated with fireflies
and from your open mouth gushed
brocaded carp. Everything inside and
around you was still alive, but your eyes
were the last to open, and tight in your grip
were silver bracelets that had slipped
from your wrists, too large after
those months of parting.

The crescent cleaved to your belly like a pepper vine.

I was there to watch you then,
as I am here to walk with you now
along this avenue of concertinaed lanterns,
in this grove where the leaves dance
with epigrams and there is no need
for mirrors to prove the always true.

Remember yourself
beneath the fissured face
of the pregnant moon.

To love is to lose, to learn the art
of afterlife.

And when you walk between shadows,
your face too becomes dismembered by light.

Flight

Once in the years of forest punishment,
a wounded bird plunged comet-like
into a purlieu I could name but never enter.

In the near distance, I watched it dip
its beak into its chest over and over again,
ripping quills from its body as if to compose

an epistle to its pain. To be winged
is to be weighted by the memory
of flight, the knowledge that

to fly at all one risks fall from grace,
for one's plumes to moult one by one
in a purgatory of impossible love,

for the sound a sword makes as it
is pulled from its scabbard to be the
last sound tail-spinning in your ears

as you plummet, the gravity of your
one unbloodied wing crashing
you to where your other lies,
a carnage of angel-feathered carrion.

Meteorite

To rewrite fate you must
be given a quill from
the wings of a fallen angel.

See how impossible love
writ the cosmos with
scars of light?

Or perhaps it was
scars of light
that writ the cosmos
with love impossible.

You choose the phrasing.
It's enough to know that
you too can survive the impact,
you too bear the weight of light.

Daughter by Blood and by Way of Sea and Sky

My mother who drank a grail of blood
squatted by the seashore and lullabied me
into a casket of sandalwood and sweet reeds.

Women have done this by dawn-light
since first doubt, first prophecy.

She pushed me forth into the tides, touched by no
water or salt that had not come from her eyes or mine.

Did she know how I would arrive back on the island,
chattel as in a dice game, an apparition, my hair black cirrus?
I swooped from the sky spilling ornaments,
spilling invectives and incantations,
spilling princess-blood from places caressed by claws.

Every crown I lost had been worn seated on a lap
– not throne I lost, but warmth of thigh.

Ask me what I knew of islands
and I will unring each key in an archipelago
of lyric-locked song, lip-latched colostrum,
scent of sudden rain in the tea-terraced mountains:

how I drew my breath in as chariot-shadow
loomed over ocean-sieged land;
how my terror made way for
memory, memory, memory.

Circle

I folded my body in two,
pressed my finger into mud

and drew it: my queenly corona,
the trajectory of my orbit,
my only perfect revolution.

storyline

bloodline

lifeline

So much came to pass in a single trespass.

I stepped across the line.
That's how I made it mine.

Halāhala

Like that blue-throated god,
I have learnt how to hold my
suffering so it trembles between
belly and breath without trickle.

All my life I have caught
every drop and arrested it thus,
and my voice has been darkened by
the bruise of its indigo.

Gondolier, go slow. The river
is deep and my vessel, full. All night
I must carry this fermata. I must
contain all of these many tidal things,
and I must swallow each one with
a dowager's unflinching grace.

Queen of the Night

I sought your counsel in the hours
others thought to be darkest,

when only I saw your writ illumined
in owl plumage, unnameable talon,

your words thundering through me
like a thing with hooves.   I praised you

even as the light spilled from my veins
when I fell from grace, milky ways of faith

     – still holding your name an amulet

against gravity, believing you could never lead
me to resurrection blindfolded. Believing.

     But here I am, igneous, unmothered,

a banished star moving through the worlds
without the benediction of a moon.

Lioness

Sister whose face
looked into my shame
with leonine splendour –

mercy and grace infinite
in carnelian radiance –
    serpents noosed in her fingers,
    stars thrown into disarray
with a shake of her mane –

her body obsidian,
human.

There in the dust
of a lazuli
cavern,
it was my self
she taught me to fight.

Shadow and surface
interlocked like triangles
in sacred diagram.

It was my self she
taught me to honour
on the stepwell into and
    out from the sanctum

(it is intricate; my ichnites

are there for you
who seek passage).

Listen for her echo
in the abyss,

how she said:
in lieu of blood,
learn to offer
red oleander

in lieu of promises,
learn to offer the
viscera of tears.

~

into the light

step   step

by   by

step   step

out of the illusion

lok   *   world
a   *   without
loka   *   world

Nightblindness

Wildness became my familiar,
and I became its mistress,

husband of its secrets,
midwife of its charms.

I have stepped into the void, virgin one.
It gave me what it knew, and I carried
its teachings through into
the altar of the
only world.

Baptisms for the damned. The debts of bloodlines.
Now I wander the moors and intoxicate the brines,
I command the aviary of the aether
and make a bower of the sierra.

I cannot unsee what I endured
in that time of nightblindness.
    But I bore it and into it
lifetimes of raw devotion.
Now I reach into subterranean wisdom,
and every vesper still echoes back to me.

The Ascent

at the first gate   *muladhara*

ask for the thing that gives you back your heart
ask for the thing that reverses the beheading
ask for the thing that you need most immediately
because it is what you will spend years
trying to fully retrieve

      all else returns, less
painfully,
                  but take your sandals first
the path is yours alone to endure

at the second gate   *svadishtana*

ask for the thing that floods the world fecund
and then ask for the cincture that
gives you sole dominion
over your true cathedra
your battleborn sex

at the third gate   *manipura*

ask for the negotiations, the charms that
unmake the hardness of the world –
carnelian for your wrists, aventurine
to dewdrop from your ears to your clavicle,
lapis lazuli for the parting of your hair

they are not trinkets, they are talismans,
and it is their weight that will hold you
down to your body in the days and nights
when you cry out for a meaning for
your damn-delivered survival

at the fourth gate *anahata*

ask for your armour back, and let the
invectives slide from your shoulders
as you hold out your handcuffed wrists
to accept it

yes, you covered your heart
you covered it with gold
you covered it with cicatrices
that was no mistake;
ask, also, for the skeleton's key

at the fifth gate *vishuddhi*

ask for your allegiances
and count them, and count them
again: who remains, who was lost?
carve their names into the caves
                    then forget them

demand it but expect no loyalty, accept
this heartache with the consolation
    of knowing –
you who have   risen from the dead
will raise a grail of blood
at your coronation

at the sixth gate   *ajna*

ask for lucre
because the weights of justice
are illusory except in the eyes of the
longue durée   and you must fill
them in some way, the days without

you must alchemize all of this
even as all that's salvaged of you
burns and melts, burns and melts
soldering your suffering with a seal of gold

at the seventh gate   *sahasrara*

ask for everything

it was yours to begin with

but there was just no other way

I Spoke the Words

Over and over, I spoke the words.

Knee-deep in the reeds, salt-pillar,
the hooves of forgotten sins thundering
me towards an unnameable baptism.

Over and over, I spoke
the words. I drew language
from me like a trail. I drew language
from me like exorcism. I drew language
from me like a twisted helix.

Over and over, I spoke the words.
And like this, I kept from coming undone.

I pressed my knee to the corpse of my
consciousness and pulled from it
the mandrel that impaled it
illiterate.

And there in that abattoir,
I riverined back to life, and
    in me and from me
came torrents of future
and deluges of memory

and words,
and words.

Testimony

And by the time I arrived in the steppes
in that black light of revelation,
the rosettes over my breasts tattered,
the lapis lazuli at my throat a bird of captivity,

I no longer wanted to be the one
to execute my own genesis.
When I sang at that cusp of
wisdom, I did not know

if the cantos were stolen or sovereign.
I did not know if I sang or screamed.
I did not know I was weeping until
someone boughed to tell me
(*I did not know*),
her palms full of eight pointed stars
that once slept in the churn of my belly.

In transgression, I learnt where the lines were.
I drew them myself. I dragged them down
the mountain, their weight became my body itself,
its history hieroglyphed for anyone to see.

Beloved, betrayer, witness with hooded eyes,
how do I bear this, except by way of testimony?
How do I tell you, except by telling you:

How because of longing I almost died.
How because of language I lived.

Recitation

book of the forest
book of the stars
book of the earth
    and underneath

canto of origins
canto of the dynasty
canto of forest
canto of citadel
canto of beauty
canto of the island
canto of consequence

praisesong of the body
praisesong of the spirit
praisesong of the psyche

manuscript of menses
    and collyrium
manuscript of stigmata
    and vermillion
manuscript of haemorrhage
    and gold leaf

word of the unlocking
word upon release
word that gives passage
    back into the world

Benediction for the Feast

Come to my table,
    my beloveds, my betrayers.

Let me feed you from the bowl of life.

    Cross my threshold
empty of palm, open of heart, eager of belly.

I have picked only fruit already fallen
    and herb without malice and
    flesh anointed and absolved.

I have placed a carnation beside each of your knives.

Here's to the sweetness, here's to the sting
    and here's to the saltwater sacrament.

Here's to the dreaming, here's to the dead
    and here's to the sacred delusion.

Take the hollow at the centre of your being
and   prise it open   to be
    savaged by grace, to be
    alchemized by love,

to be filled with
the dark and the holy,
    the sublime and the terrible.

Bloom fierce
and wild and splendorous. Drink
    deep and without qualm. There's enough
        for us all.

Carrying Back

Through the long war I held my fire,
    even while nightmares tapped my teeth
as though they were ivory and my limbs
turned into tinder, splintering
    in the heat of desertion.

I carried my heart with me like
    a knot of reeds,
like a scarlet herring,
like someone else's signet ring.
As long as I laid no claim to it,
there was no likelihood of loss.

These are the ways of the dispossessed.

I carried knowledge with me like
    a knife, and day by day
I expurgated all that did not serve me,
all that would not let me live,
all that without which I could still live,
    until what remained was elemental,
a beacon, a long burning, a light.

Fireproof

They set the forest on fire.
They set the garden on fire.
They set the aquiline inner face
    of the foxtail orchid on fire.

There is a story they do not speak
of how I walked uncharred
through chambers of
wildfire and ash,

trying to cool the embers
with elegies of tears;

of how I was pulled
    incandescent
from inferno like
one more prisoner of war
kept alive for ransom,
paraded like a decapitation.

Without atonement,
they ululate only
    the story of how
in the end, after all smoulder

I will be buried,
not burnt,
amidst abrogations of smoke.

Torch

You promised no fire could touch me
    but behold
the burning ghat of my heart.

Self-portrait as the Island on Fire

The first place that flame touched earth was in a ring around my body. And for a moment I smiled, pleasured by that warmth, I who live within circles of my own making and undoing. Scarlet and gold. Then sound came to me: crackling. Stems and small conflagrations. A solar flare setting alight a dynasty of trees. Palimpsests elided into dark plumes. I breathed in smoke before awareness came, and with it – terror.

Sea-sieged, salt-lined but sere, the will to live and the fear of dying rising in tormented crescendo. Earth on fire bounded by water that draws only another line – the long serrated incurvation of a solitary teardrop. Beyond this no more will burn. But beyond this there is no more.

Know this: all of you can burn in isolation, the light of what you are held opaque within the eyes of those who watch, but they will neither look away nor venture closer. All of you can burn and still none will surge towards you. At the distance of the arsonist's arrow, in the shadow-smoke of ambuscade, they wait for you to turn to ash. For the blazing heart of you to raze itself out, so that they can say that you had wanted to turn to cinder, that you had always smouldered too brightly to save.

Phoenix

What if I lived
only so I could speak of this:

of we who survive damnation.

I who on the other side of selfhood
emerged a creature infernal:

mother, mud-eater,
beautiful as forest fire

*

I who have borne the unbearable,

    I who held the unspeakable
in my beak
as I tried to sing

*

I.

a line
made by a plough
on the wet body of
the earth in the guise of
a woman in the guise of
a god in the guise of
a planet in the guise of
a star in the guise of
love in the guise of war

The Amputees

When my home became a city of ruined temples,
    I portmantaued my life and waited
for the harbinger to arrive at my door. Around me,
in a language meant only for posterity, I left records
    of the gods who fled, the gods who returned
the day after the apocalypse, alone or in pairs, to
    pick their ears and noses from the wreck,
their severed limbs a blasphemy of beauty.

Their eyes were stone, their countenances terrible.

I am the woman who walked this land
long after
    her broken gods
had departed it, their shadows receding
    among the remains of their dominion.

When the harbinger came for me,
    I went without prayer.
In my belongings
    I carried as much as I could – a palm in
the gesture of blessing, the adorned swell of a breast,
the half-closed eyes of one who sees all,
salvaged none.

Fire-forged, Blood-born

the wild-haired one

At the core of every blood epic
is a woman
born of battle-lust,
the one whose
body is a weighted dice
in a game rigged by
fork-tongued grammar.

She comes through
deep magic.

*

We are proof of what happens
when a curse is inverted.
How from grail of blood
and fire-sacrifice emerge
the true twice-born,
who having transcended time,
move equidistant
between worlds.

See yourself in my eyes, soul sister,
you and I and we are She –

who holds the womb-songs of vivid stars
as she does the darkness between planets,

fire gentle as afternoon tide at her feet,
blood resplendent at the parting of her hair.

Starsong

Lover, light-bearer,

how great this gift of mine –
condemned to stray the universe,

       sister of the Pleiades,
       bloodbound to nebulae,

I have lived more deeply
than I could have
by your side.

Until I imploded,
      I did know how I could sing.

But now where once I shattered,
I linger into infinity,
radiating strung
light.

Every constellation I wander
I wander with your memory
    oscillating in me,   and in
this way I keep your praise,

and with me all the cosmos
pulses   with grace.

Scorched Earth

The end of love
is not death itself,
nor a bridge
turning the water
saffron with the
reflection of its burning.

I have made that crossing,
and I have walked my way
back not on my knees
but on singed soles,
singing,

my torch
tongue
blackened
from truth-telling.

How do you know
that nothing burnt of me
in that tribunal of sorrow?

There are darkened places in me
that were never there before, and
I rise and fall every day with a
prayer to never again know them.

No, death is nothing like the
end of love, with its tender roots
and long burning.

But we become what we endure.
So I myself am an exodus,
a pilgrimage route paved with
roses the colour of live coals.
I myself am hallowed ground.

Fire-walking

Dusk carnival,
the ocean opening her arms
as the camphor is lit,
and among the magus,
perfect concord. But

no war is over
until the last woman
stops wailing.

My fists were full of hibiscus
and under my feet the embers
were small star-stung implosions.

Where is there room for fear
in the heart of one who has held
all the love and consequence
in the known and invisible worlds?

Perhaps you who watched
with hooded eyes saw
only my pyre. But the
earth herself was dilated
beneath my seared steps.
And when I emerged from
the caldera of her womb

I was incandescent, my
heart singed bittersweet.

Genesis

When they walk through fire for
the goddess of rain,
I remember him –

first consort,
how he invoked
in me   the scent of mud.

Sunkissed earth
blooming dark
under the aegis
of stormcloud.
A love so complete
it submerged all need
to bruise footprints
on the sovereign.

      When they walk
      through fire for
      the goddess of rain,

I remember me –
first consort,

fecund
with life,
flooded lush
with story.

Sita's Tears

In the antebellum years
I wept in the wilderness
of my own faithlessness.

Now, all the wilderness
is my heart's citadel.

I hold my tears
within ponds caparisoned
by lotus leaves,

membranes of feral grace,
beneath them tamed
tempests breathing deep,
perfectly still.

Sorrowless

In this garden where women weave
bracelets of bougainvillea stems,
stabbing each thorn into a blossom
of another colour, and this sorrowless
tree rains upon me so blades of fallen
gold coronate my hair, I unlearn
lexicons of lies. A captive is a captive
even if every footstep she walks
stakes a claim on the earth.
She who is sovereign knows why
the most sacred of geometries
must never be drawn except
in impermanences:
in sand, in speech, in salt.

Last Light

And again I enter the hour
at which nothing suffices
but the memory of sunset in
the southern heartland

the light sweeping its long wing
across a terrain of brown
puddles –
          the river,

scattered and whole

the slow ascent of the
moon's painted eye from
the corner where the earth
kisses its clouded lid open

the intake of breath
across bridges, a wind
that ruffles the book of longing
wordless

scent of night blooming jasmine
volery of green bee-eaters

the great pacific hum of this evening

last light
last arc of dusk in the
    spaces between
the dance and collusion of trees

in every grove,
    a shrine.

Syzygy

There was no known map through the stars then.
They burned my eyes blue by night; and
by day taunted me with their
absence, till I learned they
moved as I wandered;
so standing still,
I caught and
drank the
light.

*

Dark
was the
endurance,
dark was the deed.
When I stormed the gates
I liberated them –
the undead, the elided.
Granted subterranean sight,
I rewrote fate, I returned alive.

*

There are no exiles without borders.
No belonging without those whose
names will only be taken
beyond the pale. Unrooted,
the forest held us.
Our burning eyes
blazed a path
to the
stars.

Return

I remember the forest – how at
the border's stillness I would
take its songs into my
mouth like a vow   before I crossed over.

Each time, a river unscripted
          but already told.

I arrive again after years of bramble,
     navigating paths bled of the same
     red earth of my bones.

This is not the dismemberment
I convulsed at the threshold in,

in those long years of banishment.

I would have received any falsehood
     but this I could never have imagined,
– this ingress, this homecoming. That

I would run through the trail
by the light of forest moon,
     a desert prodigal
offering flowers to the garden.

Nocturne with Crossed Stars

the loyal one

Hold this moonflower in your mouth,
let it nectar your listenings and silences both.
There's a hawkmoth arcing towards eternity,
its wings tipped with dark matter and stardust.
The way is dappled by the timbre of your name
in one voice or another. Who named
you, beloved? Who brought you here?

The heart is a copper drum too heavy to lift
so it rests wherever it is laid on the earth,
verdigris with love for forest and water.

Listen to its sacred tremors
on this evening of incantations.

The astronomers did not know
what proxy to hold you in place by:
shell or seed, cabochon or coin from
a place where the language
conveys no unequivocal sense of time.

Everything is happening at once
and never happens, ever or now.

Somewhere there is a bow, unbroken,
that is pointed forever at the constellations,
a string that pulses almost imperceptibly.

It only feels like an epiphany,
as thought vibrates slowly
into sound.

You must hold very still to unveil the illusion,
to know the darkness from the night,
or infer the unknown from that which is known,
or the shy star from the ones
that glitter without
giving light.

River

When you leave, take with you the way light shimmered
    gold in the river,
how the weight of what you loved swirled into filigreed
    gold in the river.

That was how it felt to me, at the eventide of the
    annihilated dream,
when I first crossed into illumination at the
    threshold of the river.

There were mapmakers before me: their footfalls fade
    tender on the earth.
Like you, they brought palms of amaryllis, asked to be
    consoled by the river.

There's a pond in the forest whose water only ripples
    where you weep.
But here, all ruptures. Let your heart flood,
    uncontrolled, into the river.

Listen: the saga unbraids. Loyalties shift, fish-dappled
    in her surge.
You can no more submerge a story than you can
    hold a river.

Carry all you can into the world, a tributary. But
    pilgrim, linger a little.
Sit a while beside me. There are renderings still
    untold in the river.

Sanctuary

Snowdrop, cobra's saffron, peepal, wild mountain cherry, teak
    Every night in the forest of punishment

Silk cotton tree, yellow ginger, baobab, clitoria, tigerclaw
    I dreamt myself a sanctuary, conjured it by force of will,

Salt reed-grass, rose apple, bird-of-paradise, starfruit, neem
    seeding that silence with a desire that tendrilled

Sirisa, woman's tongues, copal, bullet wood, kadamba
    into boughs weighted by longing, sepals calyxed by lament.

Sweet grandilla, queen sago, honeysuckle creeper, muchukunda, aster
    They called me a furrow; my heart a burial of fallen flowers.

Sapota, rusty shield-bearer, magnolia, laburnum, wild almond
    Surrounded by shadowed boscage, I held it all in contempt,

Silver oak, rain tree, mussaenda, coral jasmine, tamarind
    sieving blossoms from brushwood, milk sap from thorns.
    I dreamt

Sapphire sage, banyan, vanilla orchid, casuarina, palm
    myself a sanctuary. I dreamt myself a sanctuary.
    Wild were my powers.

After Everything

I was not born knowing
    the language of trees
or the songs of the river
and its stillborn tears.

Each was a bead I learnt
by touch, a rosary of
long tillage.

But the world has always
belonged to me,
an inheritance
– and to you
who come breeze-like,
infusing these quiet afternoons
with your susurrus,
and the succour of
tea-sweet silences.

How wild
the miracle is,
that after everything
we have come to,
we have come to

be here
still.

Gathering

Where were you when
　　the world began
to sing to you again?

One day when you had
stopped looking, she
gathered together
all the benedictions
that were your due

and decanted them
into the wild reservoir
of your life.

There were golden orb weavers
there, and calypso orchids. And graceful
monarchs who lifted their painted wings

as though the miracle of their
being weighed nothing.

The world was singing again,
an eloquence of omens.
Some of us were listening.
All of us were standing, still.

And I thought I saw you there,
at the cusp of new meaning.
You were unfurling like an atlas moth.
You were spinning like a compass rose.

And I held my hands out to you
and said, precious one,
did you ever think we'd get here?
Precious one – *listen* – we are still here.

Acknowledgements

In immersing myself in the stories of Sita, Lucifer and Inanna, I owe an enormous debt not only to texts and their interlocutors, but equally to folk songs and oral narratives, dance and theatre, rumours and dreams. Each is equally valuable to me, and I cannot name them all, but I bow in gratitude.

I am grateful to the editors of the following journals, in which some of these poems have appeared: *A Café in Space* – 'Possession'; *Barely South Review* – 'Hanuman'; *Breakwater Review* – 'The Amputees'; *Cordite* – 'Southern Cross'; *Cura* – 'Echo'; *Dr. Hurley's Snake Oil Cure* – 'Monsoon'; *Drunken Boat* – 'Mirrors'; *Kindle Magazine* – 'Firewife'; *Mandala Journal* – 'Carceral'; *Mas Tequila Review* – 'Dark Moon'; *Prairie Schooner* – 'Benediction for the Feast'; *Pratilipi* – 'Last Light'; *Poetry at Sangam* – 'Chhaya'; 'Fire-walking'; *Pyrta* – 'Halāhala'; *RædLeaf Poetry* – 'Portrait As Phoenix', 'Return', 'Shape-shifter'; *Superstition Review* – 'Distant Star' and 'Sun-swallower'; *The Nervous Breakdown* – 'Light Years' and 'Secret Theatres'.

'Gathering' was specially commissioned for the 2015 Commonwealth Day Observance held at Westminster Abbey, London.

To Adishakti, Pondicherry – Arvind Rane, Nimmy Raphel, Vinay Kumar, the many dogs and myriad trees, and most of all to VP – and to Sangam House for the Lavanya Sankaran Fellowship (2008-2009) that first took me there. To Prakriti Foundation, Chennai, for a decade of support.

To everyone at HarperCollins India who made this book possible, in particular my editor Sohini Basak, who helped me bring so much more to light.

'Sun-swallower' owes something to Laksmi Pamuntjak's 'Silent Prayer for My Daughter on Her Ninth Birthday'. My understanding of the word 'lokaloka' is owed to Kakali Bhattacharya's response to Gloria Anzaldúa's 'nepantla'.

To those who read the manuscript in parts and places over the years – I am grateful to each of you, and especially to Karthika Naïr and Sukanya Venkatraghavan for reassurance during one of the final cycles of writing.

To Manasi Subramaniam, who kept a lamp lit at the end of a tunnel.

To Nadika Nadja, Mihir Ranganathan, Harini Ravi and Anjana Raghavan most of all – who walked along the way.

ALSO BY
SHARANYA MANIVANNAN

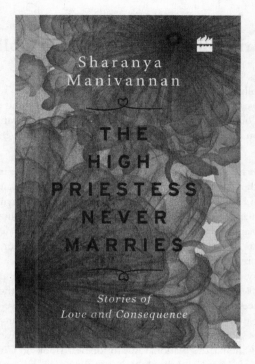

'Strung like luminous pearls, *The High Priestess Never Marries* is a collection of evocatively written short stories that feature women who seem suspended between relationships, living in moments fraught with desire and despair. Set in current day Chennai, these unnamed female protagonists cherish their independence, even within the bounds of relationships, and find their inner voices through an exploration of sensuality and choice. These are women who have accepted their many loves, their imperfect selves, and their fractured lives.'

– South Asia Laadli Media and Advertising Award for Gender Sensitivity 2015-2016 (Best Book - Fiction)

25 ▪ HarperCollins India Ltd

Celebrating 25 Years of Great Publishing

HarperCollins India celebrates its twenty-fifth anniversary in 2017. Twenty-five years of publishing India's finest writers and some of its most memorable books – those you cannot put down; ones you want to finish reading yet don't want to end; works you can read over and over again only to fall deeper in love with.

Through the years, we have published writers from the Indian subcontinent, and across the globe, including Aravind Adiga, Kiran Nagarkar, Amitav Ghosh, Jhumpa Lahiri, Manu Joseph, Anuja Chauhan, Upamanyu Chatterjee, A.P.J. Abdul Kalam, Shekhar Gupta, M.J. Akbar, Satyajit Ray, Gulzar, Surender Mohan Pathak and Anita Nair, amongst others, with approximately 200 new books every year and an active print and digital catalogue of more than 1,000 titles, across ten imprints. Publishing works of various genres including literary fiction, poetry, mind body spirit, commercial fiction, journalism, business, self-help, cinema, biographies – all with attention to quality, of the manuscript and the finished product – it comes as no surprise that we have won every major literary award including the Man Booker Prize, the Sahitya Akademi Award, the DSC Prize, the Hindu Literary Prize, the MAMI Award for Best Writing on Cinema, the National Award for Best Book on Cinema, the Crossword Book Award, and the Publisher of the Year, twice, at Publishing Next in Goa and, in 2016, at Tata Literature Live, Mumbai.

We credit our success to the people who make us who we are, and will be celebrating this anniversary with: our authors, retailers, partners, readers and colleagues at HarperCollins India. Over the years, a firm belief in our promise and our passion to deliver only the very best of the printed word has helped us become one of India's finest in publishing. Every day we endeavour to deliver bigger and better – for you.

Thank you for your continued support and patronage.

HarperCollins*Publishers*India

Subscribe to Harper Broadcast

Harper Broadcast is an award-winning publisher-hosted news and views platform curated by the editors at HarperCollins India. Watch interviews with celebrated authors, read book reviews and exclusive extracts, unlock plot trailers and discover new book recommendations on www.harperbroadcast.com.

Sign up for Harper Broadcast's monthly e-newsletter for free and follow us on our social media channels listed below.

Visit this link to subscribe: https://harpercollins.co.in/newsletter/

Follow us on

YouTube 📺 Harper Broadcast

Twitter 🐦 @harperbroadcast

www.harperbroadcast.com

Follow HarperCollins Publishers India on

Twitter 🐦 @HarperCollinsIN

Instagram 📷 @HarperCollinsIN

Facebook 📘 @HarperCollinsIN

LinkedIN 🔗 HarperCollins Publishers India

www.harpercollins.co.in

Address

HarperCollins Publishers India Pvt. Ltd
A-75, Sector 57, Noida, UP 201301, India

Phone: +91-120-4044800